A Fig for Momus by Thomas Lodge

Containing pleasant Varietie, Included in Satyres, Eclogues, and Epistle's

As can be easily understood presenting an exact chronicle of the facts in the life of a 16th Century playwright is often difficult. Thomas Lodge is no exception.

Thomas Lodge, born around 1558 in west Ham, was the second son of Sir Thomas Lodge, the Lord Mayor of London, and his third wife Anne.

Lodge was educated at Merchant Taylors' School and thence to Trinity College, Oxford; taking his BA in 1577 and his MA in 1581.

Lodge, disregarded his parents career wishes in order to take up literature. When the penitent Stephen Gosson published his Schoole of Abuse in 1579, Lodge responded with Defence of Poetry, Music and Stage Plays (1579 or 1580). His pamphlet was banned, but appears to have been circulated privately.

Already in 1580 Lodge had published a volume of poems entitled Scillaes Metamorphosis, Enterlaced with the Unfortunate Love of Glaucus, also more briefly known as Glaucus and Scilla.

Lodge seems to have married his first wife Joan in or shortly before 1583, when, "impressed with the uncertainty of human life", he made a will. That his family viewed his conduct at the time with disdain may be noted by the absence of his name from his father's will in 1583.

The marriage of Lodge and Joan produced a daughter, Mary. However, without an income from his family Lodge would have to provide it by other means.

The debate in pamphlets between Lodge and Gosson continued with Gosson's Playes Confuted in Five Actions; and Lodge retorting with his Alarum Against Usurers (1585)—a "tract for the times".

That same year, 1585, he produced his first tale written in prose and verse, The Delectable History of Forbonius and Prisceria.

Lodge appears to have been at sea on a number of long voyages. Usually these are described as 'freebooting voyages', an interchangeable term also used for piracy and plunder. Many nations endorsed these tactics and it seems fairly safe to suggest that these voyages were a source of revenue which would keep Joan and Mary with their heads above water. These long voyages also provided something else that Lodge would have been keen to gather and usefully use; time. During the expedition to Terceira and the Canaries (around 1586), to set aside the tedium of his voyage, Lodge composed his prose tale of Rosalynde, Euphues Golden Legacie, which, printed in 1590, would later be used by Shakespeare as the basis for As You Like It.

Before starting on his next voyage, this time to South America, Lodge published a historical romance, The History of Robert, Second Duke of Normandy, surnamed Robert the Devil; and he left behind him for publication Catharos Diogenes in his Singularity, a discourse on the immorality of Athens (London). Both appeared in 1591.

By now Lodge was on a voyage with Thomas Cavendish to Brazil and the Straits of Magellan and would only be able to return home in 1593. Whilst he was travelling another romance in the manner of Lyly, Euphues Shadow, the Battaile of the Sences, appeared in 1592.

At either end of this voyage Lodge appears to have worked on some dramas, most notably with Robert Greene.

It is thought that in 1590, together with Greene, he wrote A Looking Glass for London and England (published 1594). He had already written The Wounds of Civil War (produced perhaps as early as 1587, and published in 1594, and put on as a play reading at the Globe Theatre on 7 February 1606), a good second-rate piece in the half-chronicle fashion of its age.

His second historical romance, the Life and Death of William Longbeard (1593), was more successful than the first. Lodge also brought back with him from the new world voyage A Margarite of America (published 1596), a romance between a Peruvian prince and a daughter of the king of Muscovy interspersed with many lyrics.

The composition of Phillis, a volume and an early sonnet cycle sequence (an increasingly popular format in Elizabethan times), was published with the narrative poem, The Complaynte of Elsired, in 1593.

A Fig for Momus was published in 1595 and gained him the accolade of being the earliest English satirist. This work contains eclogues addressed to Daniel and others as well as an epistle addressed to Michael Drayton.

In the latter part of his life—possibly about 1596, when he published his Wits Miserie and the World's Madnesse, which is dated from Low Leyton in Essex, and the religious tract Prosopopeia (if, as seems probable, it was his), in which he repents of his "lewd lines" of other days—he became a Catholic and engaged in the practice of medicine, for which Wood says he qualified himself by a degree at Avignon, in France, in 1600. Two years later he received the degree of M.D. from Oxford University.

Early in 1606 he seems to have left England, to escape the persecution then directed against the Catholics; and a letter from him dated 1610 thanks the English ambassador in Paris for enabling him to return in safety.

At some point in his later life Lodge appears to have married again. This time to Jane Aldred, the widow of Solomon Aldred, at one time a Roman Catholic agent of Francis Walsingham in Rome.

From the early 1600's Lodge appears to have written or published sparingly. His later works include A Treatise of the Plague (1603) and two major translations—The Famous and Memorable Works of Josephus (1602) and The Works of Lucius Annaeus Seneca (1614), both of these went through several editions.

Obviously with his conversion to the Catholic faith life would have been difficult and most accounts agree that he withdrew from a literary life and instead concentrated on his work as a doctor. Over the years he was increasingly recognized as a distinguished physician and finally worked from Old Fish Street in the parish of St. Mary Magdalen.

Thomas Lodge died in London, most probably during an outbreak of the plague, in 1625.

Index of Contents

TO THE RIGHT HONOURABLE AND THRICE RENOWNED LORD, WILLIAM EARLE OF DARBIE:

T. L. his most humble and devoted servant, wisheth all health and happines.

My honoured good Lord, hauing resolued with my selfe to publish certaine my poems, and knowing them subiect to much prejudice, except they were graced with some noble and worthie patron: I haue followed the example of Metabo, king of the Uolschi, who desirous to deliver his onelie daughter from all perill and danger, consecrated and dedicated hir to the sister of the sunne. So I no lesse carefull of my labors, then the king of his Camilla, with deliberate and aduised judgement, wholy devote, and offer up my poems to your fauour and protection: who being the true Maecenas of the Muses, and judiciall in their exercises, are of power to relieue my weaknes, by your worthines, and to priviledge me from enuie, though she were prest to deuoure me: If midst your generall fauour to all desert, your honour vouchsafe this particular benefite to my industrie, no day, or time, (as Tully counsaileth) shall define the memorie of your benefits, but as your noble father in mine infancie, with his owne hands incorporated me into your house, so in this my retired age and studie, my labour, lines, and whole life, shall be imployed to doe you honour and seruice.

Your Lordships most bounden in all humilitie,
Thomas Lodge.

TO THE GENTLEMEN READERS WHATSOEVER

Gentlemen, I know you wonder, that hauing so long time kept silence, I salute the world with so peremptorie a title: But if thou consider the reasons before you enter into mislike; you shall be satisfied, and I excused.

I entitle my booke (A Fig for Momus,) not in contempt of the learned, for I honor them: not in disdaine of the wel mindded, because they cherish science; but in despight of the detractor, who hauing no learning to judge, wanteth no libertie to reproue.

Who worthily deseruing the name of Momus, shall rather at my hands haue a figge to choake him, then hee, and his lewd tongue shall haue a frumpe to check me: Sheepe are soonest wooried by curdogs, because they are mild: but hee that nips him soundly, that bites him cowardly, purchaseth his owne peace, & escapes much perill.

Heraclitus intituling one of his bookes with Ponou Encomion, the praise of labour, King Ptolemey (causing all the copies to be bought,) commanded the first letter of Ponou to be put out, and called the booke Onou Encomion, the praise of the asse: But had Heraclitus begun with Ptolemey, and toucht him with cowardly flight from Demetrius, with effeminate vanity in apparell, with exceeding gluttonie, and drunkennes; with his letcherie with Agathoclea, and bawdry with Oenante, the King would rather haue given a talent to stop his mouth, then deuised (by taking away of a letter) to abuse his title. UUhere detraction is given to chalenge, it is good striking first, for whelpes that are whipt for brauling, are quicklie quiet.

This cause (gentlemen) hath drawne me to vse this title, and under this title I haue thought good to include Satyres, Eclogues, and Epistles: first by reason that I studie to delight with varietie, next because I would write in that forme, wherin no man might chalenge me with seruile imitation, (wherewith heretofore I haue beene unjustlie taxed.) My Satyres (to speake truth) are by pleasures, rather placed here to prepare, and trie the eare, then to feede it: because if they passe well, the whole Centon of them, alreadie in my hands shall sodainly bee published.

In them (under the names of certaine Romaines) where I reprehend vice, I purposely wrong no man, but obserue the lawes of that kind of poeme: If any repine thereat, I am sure he is guiltie, because he bewrayeth himselfe. For my Eclogues, I commend them to men of approved judgement, whose margents though I fill not with quotations, yet their matter, and handling, will show my diligence: For my Epistles, they are in that kind, wherein no Englishman of our time hath publiquely written, which if they please, may draw on more; if displease, haue their priviledge by authoritie. Briefly, I haue so written, as I haue read: so read, as I can judge: In which respect, if any man doubt, let him aske and I will resolue him: if any man reproue, let him looke to it, I will nip him: for as I am readie to satisfie the reasonable, so I haue a gird in store for a Railer. Finally, gentlemen as Prometheus, after he had formed his image of earth, presented it to the sunne; and Ops when she had brought forth Jupiter, (for feare lest he should be deuoured by time, figured in Saturne) gaue him in keeping to the Cureti; So I present this fraile image of my art, to take life, and light, from the sunne of your approved judgements, & desirous to commend, this infant of my wit to immortalitie, and defend it from the assaults of time, and enuie: commit, and submit it to your protection, the true Cureti of all cunning: who accepting these fragments in good worth, shall shortly receaue from me, matters both worthy regard and reading. Vale 6. Maij. 1595.

Yours as you use him,

T. L.

SATYRE I

DIgbie whence comes it that the world begins.
To winke at follies, and to sooth up sinnes?
Can other reason be alleadgd then this,
The world sooths sinne, because it sinfull is?
The man that lives by bribes, and vsurie,
Winkes (like a foxe) at lothsome letcherie;
Craft gives ambition leaue to lay his plot,
And crosse his friend, because he soundes him not:
All men are willing with the world to haulte,
But no man takes delight to knowe his faulte.
He is a gallant fit to serue my Lord
Which clawes, and sooths him up, at euerie word;
That cries, when his lame poesie he heares,
T'is rare (my Lord) t'will passe the nicest eares:
This makes Anphidius welcome to good cheere;
And spend his Master fortie poundes a yeere,
And keepe his plaise-mouth'd wife in welts & guardes:
For flatterie can neuer want rewardes.
And therefore Humfrey holdes this Paradox;
T'is better be a foole then be a fox;
For folly is rewarded and respected,
Where subtiltie, is hated and reiected:
Selfe-will doth srowne, when honest zeale reproues,
To heare good counsell errour neuer loues.
Tell pursie Rollus, (lusking in his bed)
That humors, by excessive ease are bred,
That sloth corrupts, and choakes the vitall sprights,
And kils the memorie, and hurts the lights:
He will not sticke (after a cup of sacke)
To flout his counseller behind his backe.
For with a world of mischiefes, and offence
Unbridled will, rebelles against the sence,
And thinketh it no little prejudice,
To be reproou'd though by good aduice:
For wicked men repine their sinnes to heare,
And folly flings, if counsaile tuch him neare.
Tell Sextus wife (whose shoes are under-layd)

Her gate is girlish, and her foote is splayd;
Sheele raile with open mouth as Martiall dooth:
But if you praise her (though you speake not sooth)
You shall be welcome both to bed, and bord;
And use her selfe, her husband and his sword.
Tell blear-eid Linus that his sight is cleere,
Heele pawne himselfe, to buy thee bread, and beere:
But tuch me Quintus with his stincking breath,
The dastard will defie thee to the death:
Thus, though mens great deformities be knowne,
They greeue to heare, and take them for their owne:
Find me a niggard that doth want the shift,
To call his cursed auarice good thrift?
A rakehell, (sworne to prodigalitie)
That dares not terme it liberalitie?
A letcher, that hath lost both flesh and fame,
That holds not letcherie a pleasant game?
And why? because they cloake their shame by this,
And will not see the horror what it is.
And cunning sinne being olad in Vertues shape
Flies much reproofe, and many scornes doth scape.
Last day I chaunst (in crossing of the streete)
With Diffilus the Inkeeper to meete,
He wore a silken night-cap on his head,
And lookt as if he had beene lately dead:
I askt him how he far'd, not well (quoth he)
An ague this two months hath troubled me;
I let him passe: and laught to heare his skuce:
For I knew well, he had the poxe by Luce:
And wore his night-cappe ribbind at the eares,
Because of late he swet away his heares:
But had a stranger, chanst to spie him than
He might haue deemd him for a civill man.
Thus with the world, the world dissembles still,
And to their owne confusions follow will;
Houlding it true felicitie to flie,
Not from the sinne, but from the seeing eie.
Then in this world (who winks at each estate)
Hath found the meanes to make him fortunate:
To colour hate with kindnes, to defraud
In private, those in publique we applaud:
To keepe this rule, kaw me and I kaw thee;
To play the Saints, whereas we divels bee.
What ere men doe, let them not reprehend:
For cunning knaves, will cunning knaves desend.
Truth is pursew'd by hate, then is he wise
That to the world, his worldly wit applies:
What is he wise? I as Amphestus strong,

That burnt his face, because his beard was long.

EPISTLE I

Sir, laugh no more at Plinie, and the rest,
Who in their publique writings doe protest
That birds, and beastes, (by naturall respects
And motions) judge of subsequent effects:
For I will proue, that creatures being dombe,
Haue some foreknowledge of euents to come.
How proue you that I heare some Momus crie?
Thus (gentle sir) by good Philosophie.
First brutish beastes, who are possest of nought
But fantasie, to ordinate their thought.
And wanting reasons light, (which men alone
Pertake to helpe imagination)
It followeth that their fantasies doe moue,
And imitate Impressions from aboue:
And therefore often by the motion
Of birds and beasts, some certaine things are knowne:
Hereon the Stragerite (with judgment deepe)
Discourseth in his booke of watch and sleepe;
That some imprudent, are most prouident,
He meaneth beastes, in reason indigent,
Where naitheles their intellective parts
(Nothing affected with care-killing harts,
But desert as it were and void of all)
Seeme with their maners halfe conaturall.
For proofe, the bitter stinges of fleas, and flies,
The slime-bred frogges, their harsh reports and cries
Foresignifie and proue a following raine:
How proue you that cries Momus once againe?
Why thus dull dunce: The moyst and stormie time
Fitting the frogges that dwell in wette and slime,
Makes them by naturall instinct to croke,
Because ensuing raines the spleene prouoke:
And so the fleas, and flies in their degree,
By their attracted moyst humiditie,
Drawne from a certaine vertue elative,
Whence raine his generation doth derive:
Seeke more than their accustom'd nutriment.
So cocks in season inconuenient
That often crowe, and asses that doe rub
And chafe their hanging eares against a shrub;

A following raine doe truelie prophecie,
And this the reason in Philosophie:
The cocke whose drienes by the heate was fed,
By moysture feeles the same extinguished:
The asse with vapours caused by the raine,
The humors then abounding in his braine:
Ingendereth an it thing in his head:
What neede I more, he that hath Virgil read,
(Were he as Cato, crooked and precise)
Would graut that birds, and beasts were wether wise:
But if some misbeleeuing lad there bee
That scornes here into judge, and joyne with mee:
This paine I doe inioyne him for his sinnes:
When porpose, beate the sea with eger sinnes,
And beastes, more greedily doe chaw their cud,
And cormotants, seeke shore, and flie the floud;
And birds doe bowse them in the pleasant springs,
And crowes doe ceaslesse crie, and beate their wings:
That cloakles, in a champion he were set
Till to the skinne he thorowlie be wet.

TO REVEREND COLIN

ECLOGUE I

Ergasto
Damian

Ergasto
Sing us that carroll (Damian)
Amintas soung when he began,
To follow Ringdes minstralsie,
And made us merrie melodie.

Damian
Yong lad, my strings are broke and spent,
My harpe, records no merriment,
The moderne and new fangled laies,
From auncestrie beare hence the praise;
Such strange Terpanders now professe.
To moue both mirth, and heauines,
By euery motion of the fingers,
That olde men seeme but sorie singers.

Ergasto
Let yong men boast what art they list,

Mine eares chiefe pleasure doth cōsist,
In hearing what concentfull laies
Our Fathers chaunted in their daies;
For often haue I found this true,
The sence is olde, the words be newe:
What ere the yonger boast and braue,
Their worth, & wit, from eld they haue:
Olde sence by upstarts newlie suted
In words ill warpt, is not reputed
The deede of him that formd the stile,
But his that did the sence compile.

Damian
Since thou canst argue so for age,
My voice with harpe some warre shall wage:
And I will sing thee such a lay
As erst I heard my Ringde play.
At Galateas wedding feast,
(Where sea to heare, his musicke ceast.)

Cantus
There was a time (or writers haue missung)
Wherein our partiall mothers ballance hung
With equall poise: and fish, wild beastes, and birds,
Had vse of reason, and of needfull words:
Wherein foure-footed beasts of sauadge field,
(Who sought the state of winged fowles to wield)
Conspir'd, (the better to defence their states)
To chuse the fish, to be their mutuall mates:
Who vainly trusting to their fraile defence,
Consented quickly to the beastes pretence,
Supposing nature, equallie had lent
Like force in earth, as liquid element:
Hereon (ambition egging on the flocks
Of proud foure-footed beasts) the shoares, and rocks
Were fild with fish; and heauen, with shoutes and cries,
And gastlie breathings, almost lost his eies:
When all the foules, embatail'd in the aire
(Seeing their fortunes almost in despaire)
Besought the Gods, (who all injustice hate)
To be assistant in this dire debate:
Ioue, by a thunderclap a signall gaue
Upon their prayers, they should good fortune haue,
And speedily sent out the Southerne wind
To drive the waters from their bounds assind;
A murren on the beasts he thrilled downe:
Whilst thus the reuerend judge doth threat and frowne,
The fowles they stoupe, and offering vrgent blowes,

Finde hartles beastes, and each where liveles foes:
The fish, on waueles shore disperst, and left,
Of pride, and life, were all at once bereft:
The fowles preuaild, and fed them fat with pray,
And after victors like did flie away;
And beating off the aire with open wings
They tun'd this carroll to the woods and springs,
To beasts, to fish, (reseru'd from brunt of warre)
To all, that (with both factions mortall are)
Beware (ô what soeuer race you bee)
(Too much ambitious in felicitie)
To strive to raise your fortunes through oppression,
Or count your neighbours purchase your possession,
For Gods reuenge each impious attempt
Before the plague, or punishment be drempt:
Be sure the square whereby you build your states,
Must breake and faile, in dangers and debates;
For Nemesis hath euery houre reseru'd
A plague for pride, that hath from justice sweru'd:
Oh you, whose calme, makes neighbours stormes seeme sore
Trie you your tides, before you trust your ore,
The surge may rise on sodaine ere you thinke,
And force you, (whilst you swim, secure) to sinke.
Who trustes to choice of proud confederate,
And failes in choice of faithfull friends estate;
Let him disclaime his armes, and claime foresight;
Lest he with beastes, mannage a beastlie fight.

Ergasto
In sooth this is a wittie lay
More pleasant then the verrelay,
The shepheard sings unto his sheepe
As soone as day begins to peepe.

Damian
Waigh not the words, but marke the worth,
Great flouds doe often issue forth
From humble waters, and deepe skill,
May flow from an impolisht quill.
Who waites for words, may get him hence,
For shepheards onely sing for sence.

Philides
Eglon

Philides
What wrong, or discontent, old Eglon hath with-held
Thine honorable age from gouerning the state?
Why liv'st thou thus apart, whose wisdome wont to shield
Our kingdome from the stormes of foes, and home-bred hate.

Eglon
Ah Philides, the tast of trouble I haue felt,
Mine actions misconceau'd, my zeale esteem'd impure,
My policie deceite, (where faithfullie I delt)
These wrongs, (all undeseru'd) haue made meliue obscure:
Besides, my youthfull yeares were cancel'd by mine age,
(The verie Inne of griefes, of sicknes, and of cares,)
Time bids me now prepare, with death some warre to wage
And thinke upon mine end, and shun these worldlie snares:
And time it is (God wor) when age hath got the start,
To flie from publique noyse, and brawles of judgement seate,
For now my wits waxe weake, and scarce yeeld vse of art,
My limmes are stiffe and starke, my pulses faintly beate.
And this late-purchas'd age, (besides all other paines)
Is subiect to contempts, accus'd of auarice,
And youth, with selfe conceit, hath so bewitcht his braines,
As he esteemeth yeares, wits chiefest prejudice.

Philides
Can men so farre forget the reuerence and awe,
They should in justice, yeeld to siluer-suted haires?
Is duetie so despis'd, (enioyn'd by natures lawe)
That youth impugneth age, in mannaging affaires?
Then worse then Ethnicks farre, may Christians be esteem'd,
For both among the Greeks and Romanes, I haue red,
Such honors given to eld, that nothing happie seem'd
Wherein their counsell mist, and wisedome had not led:
In Solons happie lawes, in olde Licurgus schooles,
In Numas sage decrees, and graue Prometheus books,
Amercements were set downe for such misgouern'd fooles,
As did maligne at eld, and loath their reuerent looks:
For where they first ordain'd, the Gods should be ador'd,
Next, that the silly poore, should want no due reliefe,
They lastlie, did command the yonger to afford
All honour unto age, and still to hould them chiefe:
The Romane Senate wont, in giving dignities
To take respect of yeares, of judgement, and discretion,
The Lacedemon state, in all their souerainties,
Did yeeld their publique charge, to aged mens possession:

Taught by these flouring states, by men so fortunate,
(As reading what they did, our mindes are stir'd to follow)
I wonder that our world, should so degenerate,
From perfect awe, and carrie harts so hollow?

Eglon
Ah Philides, forbeare to wonder at the time,
There must be some contempt, before a plague succeede:
I see great stormes at hand, and sigh to see them clime,
Whose fall I might bewaile, before it come indeede.
But let all reasons passe, of enuie, and disgrace,
Sufficient to with-draw, a man from common weale,
Not these alone procure, me leaue mine honored place
But this, because tis time with state no more to deale:
The houre prefixt is come, the reuolution fixt,
Wherein I must, and will, give over gouernement;
Taught by those happie men, whose weale, with sorrow mixt,
Did make them leaue the world, which danger doth present:
Oh when I sadlie thinke of olde Lucullus wit,
Who hauing fortune thrall, and fame attending him,
Thought good to leaue the world, when he had conquer'd it,
And rather cease in time, then sincke, in hope to swim:
I cannot chuse but smile, because by like aduise
I flie from froward hate, (as olde Metellus did)
And leaue ungratefull men, (as erst did Scipio wise)
Deeming it happines in private to be hid:
Had Cicero forethought, how sweet this course had beene
When he had master'd fame, and conquer'd Cateline,
His Tusculanum then, he had more often seene,
And left ungratfull Rome, before he did decline:
But hope of further fame, so fondlie him besotted,
That wrastling with lewd chance, at last he caught the fall,
And where he presuppos'd, true fame was him allotted,
There lost he his desire, his fortunes, life, and all:
His lessons make me wise; these warnings are mine armes;
Wherewith I conquer chance, and false Rhamnusias traines,
And now deere Philides, my mind no trouble farmes,
And great content is bought, with little thrift of gaines.

Philides
Thy reasons haue their waight, and so haue wonne my hart,
As I will leaue the world, and come and live with thee:

Eglon
So doing thou art wise, who from the world doth part,
Begins to trauell on to true felicitie.

ECLOGUE III

Wagrin
Golde

Wagrin
Whie sings not Golde as he whilome did
In sacred numbers, and diviner vaine,
Such hymnes, as from bace-humor'd braines are hid?
For shame revive thy mated Muse againe,
Let not ambitious ignorance forbid
Thy worthfull stile immortall praise to gaine,
Live thou to after age, and let thy fame,
Eternise thy deserts, and tell their shame.

Golde
Why should I make mine industrie a slave,
To day, and night? why should I dwell on thought
When as some scoffing ideot shall depraue
That which with trauaile learning forth hath brought:
Proud Aristarchus will the credit haue,
And beare that palme, the happier muse hath bought,
And though in furnace of true art I trie
My labor'd lives, yet scape not obloquie.

In such a world where worth, hath no rewarde,
Where all the gods, want shrines, but greedie gaine,
Where science sleepes; and ignorance is hard,
Why should I loose my sleepe, or breake my braine?
Can vertue spring that wanteth true regarde?
No Wagrin no: tis wisdome to refraine
In such an age, where learning hath no laude,
Nor needie Homer welcome, or applaude.

Sweete Muses, my companions, and repose,
Tir'd with contempts in silence now record
Your pleasures past; disdaining to disclose
Your worth to them, who wisdome haue abhord:
Make me the judge, and writer of your woes:
Whil'st senceles walles, (where I your treasures hord)
Doe heare such griefe, as were they ought but stone,
Hewd in this age, they might consume with mone.

Wagrin
Fie Golde, blame not all men for a few,

The Muses haue some friends, who will esteeme
A man of worth, and give desert his dewe:
Did Mercurie (as many wisemen deeme)
Surcease the wauering Cynthia to pursue,
His crosse aspects to arts, more sweete would seeme:
There are some fewe, (alas that they were more)
That honour poesie, and wit adore.

To these firme oakes (who boldlie can resist
The tempest of lewd tongues,) thy selfe applie,
Like juie, round about their bodies twist,
And live to them, whose fame should neuer die:
Sweeten their eares, and glut them when they list
With such nice numbers of sweete poetrie:
That reading, they may thinke, that euerie line
Refines their wits, and makes them more divine.

Golde
On these strong pillars (Wagrin) have I built,
And liv'd a while in sunne-shine of their grace,
But time (sweete friend) beleeue me if thou wilt,
Hath made them worldlie, couetous, and base,
Their niggard mindes, with golden words they gilt,
They are not as they seeme, in outward face,
To live in hope of that they meane to give,
Is to deceive our selves, and not to live.

Arts perish, wanting honour, and applause,
And where imperious neede doth tyrannise,
The holie heate, through worldly cares doth pause,
The minde, (with-drawne to studie for supplies)
Is soyld with earthlie thoughts, and downward drawes;
Hence come those dull conceits amongst the wise,
Which coy-eard readers censure to proceede,
From ignorance, whereas they grow by neede.

Oh were the world so forward to affect
The high conceits of artists as of yore,
When least deserts, were held in high respect;
Did wise Maecenas flourish still t'adore
The heauenly lines his Virgil did erect,
Or he whom Rome admir'd for wisdomes store;
Want, should not wring good wits, and this our age
For science, should with theirs, the battaile wage.

But now, these frugall patrons, who begin
To skantle learning with a seruile pay,
Make Poets count their negligence, no sinne:

The colde conceit of recompence doth lay
Their fierie furie when they should begin,
The priest unpaid, can neither sing, nor say:
Nor Poets sweetlie write, except they meete
With sound rewards, for sermoning so sweete.

Which sound rewards, since this neglectful time
Repines to yeeld to men of high desart,
Ile cease to reuel out my wits in rime,
For such who make so base account of art:
And since by wit there is no meanes to clime,
Ile hould the plough a while, and plie the cart,
And if my muse to wonted course returne,
Ile write, and judge, peruse, commend and burne.

Wagrin
A better mind God send thee, or more meanes,
Oh woudst thou but conuerse with Charles the kind,
Or follow haruest, where thy Donroy gleanes,
These thoughts would cease: with thē thy muse should
A sweet conuerse: then this conceit which weanes (find
Thy pen from writing, should be soone resignd.

Golde
I rest resolu'd, if bountie will, I wright,
If not, why then my muse shall flie the light.

TO MASTER SAMUEL DANIEL

ECLOGUE IV

Deliuorus
Felicius

Deliuorus
Felicius, nourish not these sullen vaines,
Live not, as if thou lothedst to impart
Unto the world thy wisdome and thine art:
Vertues obscur'd, yeelds small, and sory gaines
But actively imployd, true worth retaines:

Now clattering armes sound terror in our coast,
Like aged Nestor guirt thee in thy steele,
Win fame by valour, let impugners feele,
That though sweete Mercurie delights thee most,
Thy courage, with thy yeares, thou hast not lost:

Felicius

Eld is ordain'd to counsell, youth to fight;
Age to fore-see, young courage to enact,
High courage with true wisdome euer backt,
Winnes perfect fame: youth doth deserue by might,
But old age, by good counsell, and foresight.

Deliuorus, when as thou dost beholde
Felicius sitte apart, be thou assur'd
His mind still works: and what thou hast endur'd
In bloudie brunts, the same though being olde
He doth endure, and more a hundreth folde.

I trauaile in my soule, when thou doest sleepe
I for my countrie combate by fore-cast,
And how by day, the danger shall be past
By night I studie: Thus by care I keepe,
What hed-strong youth might loose, & loosing weepe.

I live not then obscurely, as I seeme,
But as the master of the ship performes
Far more then cōmon yonkers in great stormes,
So guiding of our states well may I deeme,
I doe, and merite more, then most esteeme:

Deliuorus

As if a life deuoted unto ease,
And mannaging affaires by policie,
Might be compar'd for worth, & dignitie
With honorable armes, by land and seas?

Felicius

Why not (sweet friend) yeeld reason if you please?

Deliuorus

Whom euer did the rising sunne behold
More royalliz'd, and dignified then him,
Whose glorie, (though fell fortune sought to dim)
His courage rais'd, his conquests manifold,
Commaunding all, himselfe still uncontrol'd?

By armes, Realmes, Empires, monarchies are wonne,
To armes, lawes, justice, magistrates submit,
Arts, sciences, before their triumphes sit,
And beg their grace, and sing what they haue done,
Amas'd to see the race, which they haue runne.

Felicius

Deliuorus, warre, honour doth deserue,
Yet counsell in all kingdomes policied
Is farre more worthie, and more dignified:
For armes, but in extreames doe neuer serue
To reconcile, and punish such as swerue.

First haue an eie to Grecian gouernements,
And euen in them, the truth will be explain'd:
In Athens, where Themistocles remain'd,
Though much he conquer'd by his regiments,
Yet Solon, was more prais'd for his intents:

Themistocles, by armes; he by good lawes:
One, conquered foes, the other planted frends;
One got the wealth, the which the other spends,
Both fame: though not like measure, nor like cause:
For counsell to it selfe more honour drawes.

Pausanias, and Lysander by their swords,
And warlike vertues, made Laocena ritch,
Fame followed them where they their tents did pitch,
But graue Licurgus, by his lawes and words,
Did merite more, then these renowmed Lords,

Though these attempted, he prefixt the way,
Though they commanded, and arraung'd the bands,
Licurgus put the fortune in their hands:
Though Marius could begin, and make the fray,
Yet Scaurus policie deserues the bay:

Let Catulus, with Pompey be compar'd,
Or wittie Cicero, with Cateline:
And to preuent with policie diuine
That which the other ouer rashlie dar'd,
Deserues such fame as may not be impar'd.

Say militarie vertue doth require
A valiant hart, great strength, and constancie:
The selfe-like guiftes in ciuill policie
Are requisite for such as doe aspire,
To gaine renowne by counsell for their hire:

In briefe, for what is warre ordain'd but peace?
And perfect peace is end of bloudie warre:
And sith the ends, fore-meanes, is prised farre;
Let warre, his boast of dignitie surcease
And yeeld to wisdome, which doth peace encrease.

Peace, doth depend on Reason, warre on force,
The one is humane, honest, and upright,
The other brutish, fostered by despight:
The one extreame, concluded with remorse,
The other all injustice doth devorce.

Deliuorus
Felicius thy reasons are approu'd
(If measured by the square of statemens skil,
Who on their bookes hang their opinions still)
But I, who from my youth the warres haue lou'd,
From mine opinion may not be remou'd.

For by that methode which my selfe haue tried
I find such word-bold warriors as you be
As fit for warre, as apes for minstralsie:
For what can you prescribe, or els prouide,
To order those, whom you could neuer guide?

Thinke you Vigetius serues to make you fit
To give directions to a generall?
No book-men no, time now hath changed all,
Both men, and meanes: war craues a greater wit
And courage, then when Rome directed it:

Should we exspect, (as erst the Romaines did)
Instructions to dislodge, encampe, assaile,
Before we did endeuour to preuaile,
The meanes to conquer would be lost, and hid:
Basely fights he who warres as others bid.

All things are chang'd, the meanes, the men and armes,
Our stratagems now differ from the old,
Expert in booke, was neuer trulie bold,
Demosthenes, whose tongue the souldier charmes,
Fled coward-like away in hot alarmes.

This said, he ceast, and would no more proceed,
Felicius left him setled in this thought,
I, hearing both the reasons they had brought,
Resolu'd that both deserue true fame indeed,
And pray that wit may thrive, & war may speed.

TO F. M.

SATYRE III

It is as common as unkind a fault
In youth, (too subiect to this worlds assault)
To imitate, admit, and daylie chuse,
Those errors, which their lawles parents vse.
For what by vaine example youth conceaues,
The same for lawfull, daily he receaues,
If damned dice the father doth affect,
The selfe-like follie doth his heire infect,
If lust; to lust the sonne is too proclive,
If fraud, by fraud his wanton race will thrive:
If surfet, surfet is esteemd no sinne,
For youth perseuers, as he doth beginne.
And where to natures, (forward to retaine)
Lewd obiects are annext and customes vaine,
The wounds grow desperate, & death doth end,
Before good counsell can the fault amend;
Lucillas daughter, she that keepes the swan,
That saw her mother dallie with her man;
Steale privy sports, for sweet meates hazard fame,
Scarce twelue yeares old begins to do the same:
For nature, ioynd with custome, neuer failes
But by her selfe, and in her helpes preuailes:
And why? because what children apprehend
The same they like, they follow and commend:
And where the mind is willing and addict,
Th'examples are more forcible and strict:
And though some natures, by especiall grace
Correct themselues, and give not follie place,
Yet leane the most part, to example so,
That what they like, they hardly can forgoe:
Then (gentle friend) frō damned deeds abstaine,
From lawles ryots, and from pleasures vaine,
If not regarding of thine owne degree,
"Yet in behalfe of thy posteritie:
"For we are docible to imitate,
Depraued pleasures tho degenerate.
Be carefull therefore lest thy sonne admit
By eare, or eie, things filthie or vnfit,
Exclude the bawd, the parasite, the whore,
The dicer, drunkard, swearer from thy dore,
For such contemptible consorts as these,
Leaue ranckest poysō where they sweetly please
And as thy child resembleth thee in face,
In foote, in feature, and in outward grace,
So studie thou (thine actions being good)
He may wax like in maners, as in blood:

If thou espie within thy curious knot,
Some tangling twitch, that doth thy flowers rot,
Or in the picture hanging in thy hall,
That represents Caesar maiesticall,
Thou see some spots that spoyle and doe disgrace
The matchles modle of thy monarcks face,
Wilt thou not quickly roote away the one,
And wipe the other from the piece anone?
So in thy sonne demeane thy selfe likewise,
If thou perceive a sinne, that doth disguise
And choake the beauties of his toward mind,
If in this image of thy selfe thou find,
Corruption, choaking vertue, error grace,
And will, vsurping reasons rightfull place:
Disswade by fatherly admonishment,
Schoole, and correct, aduertise, and preuent:
Make him by gouernment, and perfect zeale,
A happie member of his common weale,
And not by negligence, and libertie,
A scouge unto thy private familie:
The eaned lambe doth loose that colour seld,
The which at first, thingendring ewe beheld:
The stained cloth, retaines his grayned die,
The Ivory his first Imagerie,
The bird but scarcely broken from his shell,
Feeds on that food which first he liked well;
The tunne retaineth long, the tast, and sent,
Of that pure licour which at first it hent:
And what impressions we in youth retaine
In age, our reason hardly will restraine:
The idle More, the Turke, the Saracen,
The Chinois, and the wealthie Abissine:
Obserue that custome, and idolatrie
Which was ingrafted in their infancie;
Then in the presence of thy toward heire
Beware to frisse, currle, and kembe thy haire,
To spend three houres, in gazing in a glasse,
Before thy wife and daughter goe to masse:
Take heed thy gagtooth'd hostes in his sight
Tell not how oft she tyres thee euery night,
Beware thy sonne doe neuer heare thee bragge,
That thou hast paid twelue angels for a nagge,
And pawn'd it to the rich and broking bawd,
For whores, and capons, little to thy lawd:
Take heede the toward had doe neuer heare,
That thou hast spent a thousand pound a yeare,
Take heed thou neVer sweare whilst he is by
That thou by othes darst proue an open lye,

Lest seeing thee make light of lothsome sinne,
To practise like misdeeds he doe beginne;
And thou at last to thy excessive griefe,
Behold thy selfe a begger, him a theefe:
For by a fatall law it comes to passe
That lewdnes is defam'd and euer was.
And life corrupt by unexpected shame
And timeles death is buried with defame:
Enough, if grace be gone, then words be vaine:
Ile tell thee more if so I write againe.

EPISTLE II

Bolton, amidst thy many other theames
Thou dost desire me to discourse of dreames:
Of which, what I could gather, reade, or find,
I here set downe to satisfie thy mind:
Dreames then (in sleep our spirits true retreate)
Do chalenge their predominance, and seate:
And in their natures, are but fantasies
Made by the motion of Imageries,
According to the sleepers habitude
Of euery sensible similitude.
So then, all dreames from divers causes grow,
And from th'interior, or th'exterior flow:
Thinterior likewise hath a double right,
The one is mentall, clayming by the spright,
Where through in sleep (the fantasie and thought
Encountring) strange and rare effects are wrought;
Resembling those, which our affections kept,
And thoughts did trauel on before we slept:
The other cause takes his fruition,
And being from the bodies disposition:
For by th'interior habitude and state
The bodie houlds, (corrupt or ordinate)
Some motion in the fancie is maintain'd,
According to the disposition gain'd:
For where as chilly humors doe abound,
Men seeme in snow, or water, to be drown'd:
This makes the sage Phisitian to coniect
By dreames, what griefes the inward parts infect;
Th'exterior cause likewise, we double call,
The first divine, pure, and spirituall,
Whereby things hidden, sacred, and concealed,

By God, or by his Angels, ere reuealed:
The next is meerely corporall; whereby
Not onely mind and working fantasie
Is chang'd, (according as the sleepers thought
Or fancie, by contaging aire is wrought)
But by th'impression of celestiall raies,
Which doe conforme affection to their waies.
For so the staid star-gazers doe areede,
That from celestiall bodies doe proceede,
The cause, & workings of our dreames in sleepe:
And in this point a mightie coyle they keepe.
Note me the houre (sayth one) and bring it me,
I will expresse th'effect and dreame to thee:
For as when choller swarmes in breast or hed,
Men dreame of things inflam'd, and fierie red,
And whereas fleugme preuailes, abounds and springs.
We dreame of watrie, colde, and frostie things:
So heauen may by his influence bestowe
The knowledge of th'effects which he doth owe,
And what in strength, and vertue it containes,
Infuse in man, in whom his worke remaines:
But by their leaues; tis not materiall
The heauens can doe onely but casuall:
But now me thinks Apollo puls mine eare
And claimes mine industrie an other wheare:
Speaking in thee, (because in thee he raignes)
And bids me busilie imploy my braines,
And prove of spirits either good or bad,
In formes, and certaine apparitions clad,
Can further force, or els infuse by right,
Unfained dreames, to those that sleepe by night.
To which mine answer is affirmative,
Because the fathers make it positive:
For dreames both true, & certaine, now & then,
By blessed sprites, are powr'd in living men
Either as pertinent to their reliefe,
Or to represse their frends impendent griefe,
Such was the dreame Albertus Magnus had,
Who whilst the world in nights-dark-cloake was clad,
Suppos'd he sawe, (neere to a water-mill
By which a brook, did flow with murmure shril)
A pretie lad, hard by the river side,
That from the bancke fell headlong in the tide,
Whilst wrastling there he lay, and he in dreame
In pittie seemd to saue him from the streame,
The morne arose, he walkt, and scarce araid
Beheld a wofull mother quite dismaid;
That piteously perplext, and tir'd with teene,

Complain'd no lesse thē he in dreame had seene.
The selfe-like hap to Nicons sonne befell,
Who knowing neither purge, not hidden spell,
To cure his patient trauel'd with the spleene,
Fell fast asleepe within a medow greene:
Wherein he thought, some spright, or genius good,
Enioyn'd him presently to let him blood
Betwixt the wedding finger and the small,
Which wakned he perform'd, and therewithall
The sicke man got his health, he wonne the same,
And thus by dreame his doubt he ouer came:
If then the heauenly bountie by good sprights,
Direct mens actions to their best delights,
To bodily contents, to perfect health,
To safetie, to securitie, and wealth:
Farre and more working is his heau'nly power,
In sending holy spirits euery howre;
Who in our mortall, and spirituall weale,
Are prest syncere instinctions to reueale:
So in a dreame King Salomon the sage,
(Both wealths, & wisdomes, wonder in his age)
Had speciall counsaile how to beare a hand
In gouerning his people, and his land:
So euen the most corrupt and unretir'd,
Haue to good ends, beene faithfully inspir'd:
So Pharao, and Nabuchadonsor;
The caitife Caiphas, and many more,
To their confusion haue fore-knowne their fall,
And miseries God threatned them withall:
From euill messengers the sonnes of pride,
To euill men, true things are tould beside,
Not for the divels tongue they shuld beleeue,
But that in right he labours to deceive,
Not for desire to manifest misdeede,
But to himselfe more faith and trust to breede.
So Socrates, the night before he sawe
Diviner Plato, skild in natures lawe,
After digestions howers were ouerpast,
And vapours in the braine digested fast,
Bethought him in his dreame that he beheld
A milk-white swan, whose pleasant note exceld,
That from the earth to heauen did singing flie,
And cheere all other birds with melodie:
Which when he wak'd, he knew fore-tould the truth
Of Platos worth; for seeing of the youth:
Here is (quoth he) that swan that sung so sweete,
Whose eloquence, all Greece shal grace & greete:
Thus much for dreames, though more remaines to say:

My Muse commaunds me now make holiday:
And end abruptly, vowing faithfully,
To prosecute this subiect seuiously.

TO A DEERE FRIEND LATELY GIVEN OVER TO COVETOUSNESSE

SATYRE IV

I heare of late (but hould it verie strange)
(That such vaine newes is common in the change)
How being old, and drawing to the graue,
Thou waxest greedie, and desir'st to saue:
As if thy life of sorrowes had no store,
But thou in policie shouldst purchase more?
Alas for thee, that at thy iournies end
Art growne so neere and carefull what to spend.
Looke on thy selfe, age hath thee by the backe,
Thy haires are white, which erst were frisseld blacke:
Thine eies are suncke, thy cheeks are leane and pale,
Thy lips are blew, thy breath is stincking stale,
Thy grinders gone, thy ghastlie gout, and murre;
Do breake thy sleepes, and scarcely let thee sturre:
Thy memorie is dul, and wel nie dead,
Thy tongue alreadie faulters in thy head:
Where al these torments make thee loth thy self,
Why art thou now enamored with thy pelfe?
Think'st thou the purchase of a niggards name
Is not a prejudice unto thy fame?
Marke me a miserable mysing wretch,
That lives by others losse, and subtle fetch,
He is not onely plagu'd with heauines,
For that which other happie men possesse,
But takes no tast of that himselfe partakes,
And sooner life, then miserie forsakes:
And what in most aboundance, he retaines
In seeming little, doth augment his paines:
His trauailes, are suspitions backt by feare,
His thoughts distraught incessant troubles leare,
He doubts the raine, for feare it raise a floud
And beare away his houses, and his good,
He dreads his neighbours cattle as they passe,
For feare they stay and feed upon his grasse,
He hides his treasures under locke and kay,
Lest theeues breake in, and beare his bags away:
Onely unto himselfe, for whom he spares,
He gathers nothing but continuall cares:

His eie disdaines his hungrie bellie meate,
Himselfe repines, at that himselfe doth eate,
Though rents increase, he lets his body lacke,
And neither spares his bellie nor his backe:
What on him selfe he laies, he houlds it lost,
What on his wife, he deemes unthriftie cost,
What on his heires, his miserie and misse;
What on his seruants, ryotting it is.
Thus from himselfe, his couetous desire
Doth draw himselfe, and on his hart doth tire:
So lives he to the wretched world alone,
Lothsome to all that long to see him gone:
If such he be, (as such he is indeede)
And far more worse, (if wealth more worse may breed)
For shame from such a sinne thy life exempt,
That makes thee rich in nothing but contempt,
They say the many packs before thy doore,
Are but the pawnes, and wages of the poore,
They say the buildings which thou dost begin,
Are rich without, but yeeld no rest within;
They say thy deerest friends are sure to pay
Great forfeitures, and if they misse their day:
They say the interest of tenne a yeere
Is held too little to maintaine thy cheere,
And yet thy selfe, thy wife, thy maid, thy knaue,
Scarce butter'd turneps upon daies haue,
They say at New-yeares-tide men give thee cakes,
And thou the next day sels them for their sakes,
They say thou sel'st the chipping of thy bred
For feare thy seruants should be ouer fed,
They say one horse may beare thy houshould stuffe,
Where for thy coyne three carts are not enough;
They say thy welted gowne, and ruffes of lawne,
When thou wert warden last was but a pawne:
They say thy plate is forfeited and lost
For halfe the money that at first it cost,
They say thy wives cast kertle is become
A paire of breeches to enskonce thy bum.
Briefly, they say that for the world thou art
Too wretched, and for God too false in hart.
All these reports thou knowest as well as I
Spring frome grounds, things fould by common cry
Are quickly sould, men hardly stop the noice
Of slanders published by common voice:
If these be true, reforme them; if untrue,
Take them for warnings what thou shouldst eschue:
What ere they be, now thinke upon thy graue,
And leaue thy worldly drudging to thy knaue,

And let him carrie fier unto thy stils,
And tend thy brewhouse, watch, & ward thy mils,
Looke to thine apples, lest they rotte away,
Set up thy hop-powles, and thy champions lay.
And thou thy selfe safe wrapt in cloth and furre,
Fall to thy prayers, desire no more to sturre,
Give to the poore, what thou hast got by wrõg,
For be assur'd thy daies cannot be long:
Follow this frendly counsell which I give,
Or els in shame, and hatred thou shalt live,
Or dead, those passengers that spie thy graue,
Shall say here lies a broking bribing knaue.

SATYRE V

In every land from Gades to Ganges flood
Too few they be that thinke upon their good:
Too few that by discretion can discerne
What profite rightly doth themselues concerne.
Behould ambitions true begotten sonne,
Spent in desire before his hope be wonne,
Striving for kingdomes which are sooner lost,
Then kept, desir'd, then had, with mightie cost.
Ending like him that senceles in his harmes
Doth strive to stem a sea with two weake armes,
Behould a mind pressing beyond his might,
Catching at stars censur'd by ouersight.
Like him tha eger scales a mountaine steepe,
And headlong fals into the valley deepe:
There lives no man so setled in content
That hath not daily whereof to repent,
Nor can reformed wit so justly deeme,
But that it leaues true goods, for such as seeme;
Briefly, the greatest gifts whereof we boast
Are those which doe attempt and tire vs most.
Peace brings in pleasure, pleasure breeds excesse,
Excesse procureth want, want works distresse:
Distresse contempt, contempt is not repair'd
Till timeles death determine, hope dispair'd.
Warre egges the victor to desire debate,
The conquer'd to submit and serue with hate;
Leaues nothing sure though he presume to choose,
But what he keeps with hate and dread to loose:
How oft hath watching policie deuis'd
A cunning clause which hath himselfe surpris'd?
How often hath lewd fraud been set afloate?

Of purpose that his goods might cut his throate?
Who builds on strength by policie is stript:
Who trusts his wit, by wit is soonest tript.
Example be thou Hepar, who profest
A home-borne infant of our English west
Hast in that shamefull schene of treasons play
Betray'd thy selfe to death, who would'st betray:
Uolcatius that subborn'd, deuis'd, and wrought
To worke out Themis, from the place he sought:
Was laught in court, and though he were not seene,
Yet wept his follies to a woodden skreene,
Was neuer since this wretched world began
To entertaine, receiue, and nourish man.
A judgment by itselfe that neuer err'd
Or wit unwrong'd by that he most prefer'd
Trauel the world, & trauerse euery clime,
And win one houre in euery yeare of time:
Compasse what ere the sea receiveth round,
And seeke to South-ward men of under-ground:
What hast thou got if following Candies fate,
That keepst no certaine compasse in thy state:
O nought of ours, our wealth, our wit, enioy'd,
If not as ours, for vs, it be employ'd,
Thy fame declining, Tellus, not thy farme,
Thy zeale presumptuous, Dacus not thine arme:
Thy bountie Varis, not thy many bribes,
Thy silence Shanus, not thy many libes.
These are those goods whereto you ought to cleave:
The rest are good in semblance and deceave.
What then in right for good may we elect?
Such things as chalenge not by lewd respect?
Seeke not in age with Crassus such a place
As both thy life and fortune may deface:
Nor fill the sea with sailes, the earth with men
In shamefull sort, to be repulst agen.
Nor leaue the northren lands, and fruitfull Gaul,
In royall Rome, thine empire to enstall:
For seldome can presumption be enthrown'd
To live esteem'd, or die to be bemown'd.
An humble cote entapissed with mosse,
A lowlie life that feares no sodaine losse:
A mind that dreads no fal, nor craues no crowne,
But makes his true-content, his best renowne.
These are the choice contēts, the goods, the gaine
Which rightly can be ours: the rest are vaine.
If thou then see a troupe of garded knaues
Waite at Argastos heels like seruile slaues:
Be not aghast, admire not at his state,

For now the world is bent to serue and hate:
Tis true: that slaue whom Pompey did promoate,
Was he that first assay'd to cut his throate.

TO HIS MISTRESS A. L.

EPISTLE VI

In that same month wherein the spring begins,
And on that day when Phoebe left the twinnes
(Which was on Saturday, the twelft of March)
Your seruant brought a letter seal'd with starch,
Which by my soule (sweet mistres) when I op'te
And read your motion farre from that I hop'te,
Beleeue me (had not troubles tir'd me quite)
Might be enough, to make me laugh outright:
You pray me to aduise, and tell you what
Will take away your pursines and fat,
You pray me without any let, or pause,
To write of both the remedie, and cause,
And in a short discourse to let you know
The Antidote of that mislikes you so.
Well, since your beautie may, & must command
Thus briefly will I answer your demand:
Fatnes (connaturall to sicke, and hole,
Which neerest under-dwell the Northren pole)
In those by nature who enioy the same
Is passible, not prejudiz'd by blame:
That other growne by surfet, and excesse,
That choaks the vitall powers with heauinesse,
Is that (faire mistres) which you ought to flie
And that which Phisiques art may remedie:
Fatnes by nature (not immoderate)
Kils not the wit, quels not the minds estate:
But fatnes, by intemperance increast,
(When living man resembleth loth some beast,
And belly cheere with greedie gluttonie
Is held the fulnes of felicitie:
This maketh men addicted to the same,
Dull in conceit, grosse minded, worthie blame,
Of such doe Basile, Galen, Plato, write,
That fattest bellie hath the weakest sprite:
For reason, (onely made for mans behoofe)
Affords hereof this true, and certaine proofe:
Therefore are lawles belly-gods by kind
Defect in understanding, and in mind,

Because grosse blood by their disordred feede,
And swift concoction, plenteouslie doth breede:
And by this blood, grosse spirits from their harts
Ascend, and seaze upon their upperparts,
And from these spirits, spirits of the braine
A dead and loth some dulnes doe retaine,
Through which it comes, that they wax starke, & slow,
Because their spirits animall be so.
That fatnes then engendred, and engrost,
By ryot, surfet, belly cheere and cost,
Is hatefull: and that fatnes nature breeds
From good complexion, orderly proceeds:
Which prais'd, because approu'd, me thinks I heare
A saint, sweet like your selfe, harkt in mine eare,
And with a maiden blush intreat me tell
Why fatnes most doth in the bellie dwell.
Whereas the head (the master part of all)
Is fleshles, slender, prettie, round, and small?
To this, this answer mistres doe I make:
The bellie therefore fatnes doth pertake,
Because it keepes the matter of our meate,
And still containes our fatnes-breeding heate,
But for the head, it therefore is not charg'd,
With fat, or flesh, or by such like enlarg'd,
Because the heauenly workman did prouide,
That such a part, which is the bodies guide,
And is the seate, where souerainlike remaines
That reasonable power the soule containes,
Should not by flesh, be soyld, or ouerset,
For feare the works of reason should be let;
This probleme plainly opened to the eie,
It followeth thus of fatnes orderlie,
It vitiats beautie, makes a barraine wombe,
Because the bloud which Sperma should become
Is wholely turnd to fat, it hastneth age,
And houlds our appetites in vassellage:
It hinders bloud, and shortneth breathing to,
And maketh all things tedious that we do:
It causeth sownings, passions of the hart,
It makes the pulses in their places start.
Briefly, (if Auicen speake not amisse)
Grossenes the bodies lothsome fetter is,
The selfe opinion olde Pythagoras
Maintaind: who seeing once a fat man passe,
Said thus to them that did attend him then,
A loth some prison dothyond spirite pen:
This Plato knowing well, and waxing grose,
Chose out a shadie wood, and fruitfull close;

Where walking, he his schollers taught & train'd,
Which all his followers afterward maintain'd:
A world it were to reckon up, and wright,
How all those olde Philosophers do fight,
Contend, debate, decide, dispute, intreate,
Whether this fatnes come from cold or heate:
But to be short, the Synode and the sect
Of those who rightly natures works respect:
Conclude that by a double sort of heate,
Our fat is made, and moult, and so concreate.
Excessive heate dissolues, the meane makes hard;
Heate in excesse, as deeper read, award
Is that same heate, which doth ingender fat,
Heate moderate, is rightlie counted that
Which Galen tearmeth cold: By this decree
Two mightie factions thus accorded bee:
Well since these proofes the causes doe assure
Let vs debate a little on the cure:
Much sitting, and long abstinence from care,
Drinking of oylie wines, our fat prepare,
Egs, whitemeat, pottage, do increase the same,
And bring the waxing bodie out of frame:
Let therefore fat men growne by gluttonie,
(For to the rest no medcine I applie:)
Open a vaine; or if that seeme too sore,
Vse cuppings, and oft rubbings euermore,
Live in that aire, which is both hot, and drie,
Watch much, and sleeping little, hardly lie:
Walke much, and tosse, and tumble in the sunne,
Delight to ride, to hauke, to hunt, to runne,
Drinke little, gargarize, flie grosser food,
Or if some deeme a hare, or partridge good
Feede modestly thereon, and if he hath
Some crownes to spend, goe often to the bath:
Not Esculapius, were he now alive
Could better helps, or remedies contrive,
Except behoulding mightie Graedoes port,
He cut off both his legs to make him short:
Whether am I transported in discourse,
My Muse me thinks hath run too long a course.
The question is resolu'd, why faile I then
To seale this letter up, and leaue my pen?
Faith, nought but this in kindnes to desire
(My Genius of good wit) sure I require,
To count her fatnes no deformitie,
But as it is the guise in Italie,
To nourish that: for fat, slicke, faire, and full,
Is better lik't, then leane, lancke, spare, and dull.

TO HIS DEERE FRIEND H. L.

EPISTLE IV

That verie day wherein the sunne began
To visite Aries, by the Scot thy man
I did receive thy letters: and with thease
Thy guifts which in this world no better please,
Thy letters, I with letters doe reward;
But for the rest, (because the world goes hard)
Thinke not amisse, if for thy presents kind
My presents, be the riches of my mind;
For they oft read, will yeeld thee much content,
Whereas thy guifts will serue me but this lent.
But Tom saist thou what presents shall I haue?
Faith Harry counsell, how to spend, and saue,
Which counsell if thou keepe, and follow to;
None better then thy selfe shall live, or do:
First for instructions how thou shalt dispend:
Spend praiers on God, and peace upon thy frend,
Which doing, God will blesse thy crop, & plant,
And friend will helpe, if so thou hap to want:
Spend still on that may yeeld thee good, & gaine,
Spend on thy house, to tyle it from the raine:
Spend on thy horse, in trauell euery night,
For such expence, will make him fresh, and light,
Spend on thy teame, their labour gets thee bred,
Spend on thy neate, that breed, & erst haue bred:
Spend on thy sheepe, & see them worm'd and shorne:
Spend compost on thy land, that brings thee corne,
Spend on thy wife, and see her seemely clad,
For such expence in duetie must be had:
Spend on thy sonne, to get instruction,
That he may live by art, when wealth is gone.
Spend on thy seruants, paying them their wage,
And they will serue thee truely in thine age:
Spend stripes on him, whom words may not retaine,
Yet spend to mend by stroaks, but not to maime;
Thus spent, wel spent: now learne againe to saue,
Saue from the Sycophant, what he would haue;
Saue frō thy neighbour, that doth presse & pray,
To buy thy goods, and neuer meanes to pay:
Saue from th'insatiate husbandmā thy beefe,
Saue by fast locks, thy money from a theefe:
Saue by receiving strangers, and estates,

Be not at home to all, keepe fast thy gates:
Saue by forbearing companie, and dice,
Saue by well husbanding, thy graine from mice:
Saue by thy market, and thy sale againe,
Buy cheape, sell deare, thy profit quites thy paine:
Saue in thy diet, spend as thou maist get,
And lay up some for age, the rest for debt.
Briefly, so spend, as thou maist saue to buy,
So spare, as thou maist spend, and get thereby.
Thus in requital of thy kind good will,
My hart as kind, (though power be weakned stil:)
Presents great thanks, these counsailes graue, and true,
And till my next, occasion bids adue.

TO MASTER MICHAEL DRAYTON

EPISTLE V

Michael, as much good hap unto thy state,
As Orators haue figures to dilate:
As many crownes, as Alchymists haue shifts,
Briefly, so many goods, as thou hast guifts:
I heare some upstart Rymer set a gog
By writing poems on the Lician frog,
Or Tithons Grashopper growes enuious,
And will be famous with Archilochus:
Alas for them that by scurrilitie,
Would purchase fame and immortalitie:
But know this frend, true excellence depends,
On numbers aim'd to good, and happie ends:
What els hath wanton poetrie enioy'd
But this? Alas thy wit was ill imploy'd.
What reason mou'd the golden Augustine,
To name our poetrie, vaine errors wine?
Or Hierome, (deeply sighted in these euils)
To tearme it nothing, but the food of deuils?
Nought but the misimployment of our guifts,
Ordain'd for arts, but spent in shameles shifts.
Looke as the sunne-beame in a burning glasse
Doth kindle fire, where euer it doth passe,
But freely spred upon th'ingendring earth,
Egs on the spring, and kils the cause of dearth:
So poetrie restraind in errors bounds,
With poisoned words, & sinful sweetnes wounds,
But clothing vertue, and adorning it,
Wit shines in vertue, vertue shines in wit:

True science suted in well couched rimes,
Is nourished for fame in after times.
Thou then sweet friend, grieue not though folly thrive,
Fame got by it, dies ere it is alive:
Be thou a prentize to a blessed Muse,
Which grace with thy good words will stil infuse:
Oh let that holy flame, that heauenly light,
That led old Abrahams race in darke some night:
Oh let that star, which shining neuer ceast
To guide the Sages of balme-breathing East,
Conduct thy Muse unto that loftie pitch,
Which may thy style with praises more enritch.
They wash a More, they strive to drie the seas,
And plaine proud Atlas that intend to please,
By filthie words, by rayling and detraction,
Proper to Momus, and his hatefull faction:
For when they thinke they haue deserued most,
Alas saith wisdome, all this toyle is lost:
But all this while I haue forgot my text,
I must remember now, what followes next:
I haue perus'd, thy learned nines and threes,
And scan'd them in their natures and degrees:
And to thy choice, Apologie applie,
This sodaine tribute of my memorie.
And first for three, which Bartas wisely names
The first of ods, which multiplied, frames
The sacred number nine: Three doth include
The name beloued by beatitude:
Three doth expresse the lincke and union
That knitteth one to two, and two in one:
Three doth include his infinite in three,
And is the step to immortalitie:
Three hath his center of the second one,
His true beginning, and his end alone:
The true Pythagorists, (as I haue red)
Doe tearme the triangle, Mineruas hed:
And in their purifying bathing vs'd,
By threes, to sprinckle water once infus'd:
These threes so famous, are the steps to nine
Sacred unto the Muses most divine,
This number in proportions musicall
Is dissonant: and Astrologians call
The same Sinister for some secret worke;
Or hidden fate, that in the same doth lurke:
Hesiodus in his Theogonie,
Under Styx, nine fould streame doth signifie,
The discords, and complexions of mans bodie:
Pierias Michael, if thou list to see,

Will tell thee more, this shall suffice for me.
Here must I needes abruptlie make an end,
Call'd to discourse with old Amintas frend,
When he is gone, and I get time to wright:
Thou shalt haue more, til then sweet friend goodnight.

IN PRAISE OF MISTRIS DOGGE

EPISTLE VI

Madam, my Muse wing'd by your kind request,
To praise a dog hath solemnly profest,
And for reward, desires no further grace,
Then for a night to grant me Pretties place:
Oh you hie eies the worth of my discourse,
Succour my Muse to end her vowed course:
Diviner Plato, first (under pretence
To teach the souldier faith, and diligence)
Compares him to a dogge, that ceasles keepes
His masters tent, and chamber, when he sleepes:
That howles when he is sicke, that barkes, & bites,
When as accurst by wrongs, he eger fights:
The Greeks, and Latines, lou'd these creatures so,
That in their publique sessions to and fro,
They let them passe, where men of better sort,
Were not permitted freely to resort:
The ancient houshould Gods for ornament,
Wore dogskins on their backs: to this intent,
To signifie that as the spaniell baies,
When as the theefe his masters dore assaies:
So they, when dangers should the house attempt,
Propitious, should pursuing plagues preuent.
Them Cicero admir'd, them Aegypt lou'd,
And by their Hirogliphique signe approu'd.
The dignitie of perfect confidence,
And courage scorning inconuenience:
The Bactrians, and the Caspians, by their dombes,
In life made them their mates: in death their tombes.
Th' Aegyptians, in their sacred letters place,
A dog distraunged of his head, and face,
Fore-tokning by the same obedience due,
To louing masters, by their seruants true:
Nor can that fained folly winne regard,
Wherein the former poets did award:
Life-taming Aconite to Cerberus:
Nor can the storie of Heraclitus,

Be held for true, whereby in spaniels skorne,
Tis published, that he by them was torne.
But of their faith, what stories cannot boast?
Lisimachus, when as his life was lost;
And funerall prepar'd, and herse arrai'd,
And faire addrest, & frends with griefe dismai'd;
Began to burne his corse with many teares,
His faithfull dog that seru'd him many yeares,
In selfe same fire, that burnt his kingly corse,
Consum'd to dust, freely without inforce:
Zantippus sayling from th' Athenian strand,
Was follow'd by his faithfull hound to land:
And Philips sonne (as Theopompe doth wright)
In faithfull Pertha tooke so great delight,
That being dead, who gaue him so much game,
He built a towne in honour of his name:
The Ptamphuonians on the Afrique coast
Do reuerence the faithfull spaniell most,
And setting light by other living things,
Midst them, elect and chuse their crowned Kings.
The stout Uenetians being in disgrace,
With Clement Pope of Rome a certaine space,
By no submission, could remission gaine,
Till their Embassadors tied in a chaine
Crept dog-like under table, where he sat,
And by this meanes their publique pardon gat:
Nor is it womanish to aid, or helpe,
To combe, to currle, to feede a prettie whelpe,
Since all the kings of Persia, where they eate,
Play with their dogs, & kindly give them meate:
Thus for your dog, my doggrell rime hath runnne
no common course, wherein if I haue done
Ought pleasant to your eares, thanke both your eies,
Which are the Load-stars of my poesies.

THE ANATOMIE OF ALCHYMIE

EPISTLE VII

Thou dost desire, (and hast deseru'd farre more,)
To gather my opinion in my Rimes,
In what regard I hould that hidden lore,
Ycleped Alchymie these latter times:
To satisfie this expectation,
Sweet frend conceive much matter, in few lines,
This fruite of foolish innouation

Is first condemn'd by deepest-red divines,
Not as an art, but as the seale of shift,
The persecution of natures power,
Divine in show, in proofe, a subtill drift,
To cousen slight-beleeuers euerie hower:
For if with iealous eies we justly prie
Into the scope, and issue of the same
Nature, (the mistres of Philosophie)
Is lost herein, and wanteth power, and name:
The artists, and the practizers hereof
Resemble Cacus creeping from his den,
The common subiects of each publique scof,
The refuse race, of labour-tyred men.
Their purpose is to drag out by the eares
A quint-essence to fixe and fashion gold.
To cloth decrepit age with youthly yeares,
To quicken plants by nature fruitles old,
But al these promis'd mountaines proue a mouse,
These silly idiots plie the fire so fast;
That sodainly they blow up man and house,
And both their wealths, & wits, & fortunes wast:
Yet these quark-saluers for a colour sake
Pretend some physicall experiments,
And mightie cures with boldnes undertake,
But all their science is but complements:
They by their words enritch beleeuing sots,
Whereas in deede they emptie all their chists,
And where they promise gold, by glutting pots,
They beg for groats, and part with empty fists:
And as along the shores of Cicely,
The Syrens charme by their enchanting noates
The passengers to seeke their ieopardie,
So these by bootles hopes, do cut mens throates:
So that this studie, (as some writers deeme)
Is but a pleasing madnes at the best,
Drawn on by dreames, & thoughts of things which seem,
Till richly left, be poorely dispossest:
The fauorites of this too fond conceite,
At last through losse of substance, and of time,
Robb'd, and bereft of rent, and olde receite,
Are like a crased clocke, that cannot chime:
Olde, clothles, meatles, smelling brimstone still,
Besmeer'd with cole-dust, from their furnace brought,
Plagu'd with the palsie, (letchers common ill)
By tempring of quick-siluer quickly cought:
Their riches are the droppings of their nose,
Where els beside, the slaues are brought so low;
That for three farthings they will beg, and glose,

And sel their soules, & teach what ere they know.
In briefe, when other subtill shifts doe faile,
They fall to coyning, & from thence by course
Through hempen windowes learne to shake their taile,
And loue to die so, lest they live farre worse.
But soft sir swift (cries one) and puffes with ire,
And cals me prating knaue, that speake so large
Of such a sacred thing, which (but the fire)
Is compact quickly with a little charge:
Yea, when the Grecian Calends come (quoth I)
For why? Philosophie nere knew this are,
But some vaine upstarts, (sonnes of subtletie,
As Giberis, and witles Salesart,
Bacam, and Hermes father of this fraud,
Began the same in termes, and words obscure,
(To studious of deceit and foolish laud,)
Hoping by toyes to make their craft endure:
But let vs marke their misteries and spels
Their vaine Aenigmata and Problemes darke.
First aske they where the flying Eagle dwels,
Next of the dancing fooles, craft coyning clarke,
Then of the Lyon greene, and flying hart.
Next of the Dragon, swallowing his tayle,
Then of the swelling toade, they prattle art,
Next of more blacke, then blacke, they chose to rayle,
Then of the crowes head, tell they waighty things,
And straight of Hermes seale, they sighing speake,
Some of their Lutum sapientiae sings,
Thus on these toies, their bitter iests they breake.
Alas, alas, how vanitie hath power
To draw mens minds from vertue, under hope
Of fading treasures? Danaas golden shower
Doth rauish wits, and leades them from their scope:
Yet unto Artists will I sing a saw,
Perhaps may smell of art, though I haue none,
Wherein by reasons light, and natures law,
Ile dreame of beeing, which they build upon,
There is a thing in substance full compleate,
Not wholely earthly, nor inflam'd too much,
Not simply watrie, though it water eate,
Not sharpest, nor yet dullest in the touch,
A qualitie light felt, and apt in curing,
And somewhat soft, at least wise not too hard,
Not bitter, but in tast some sweet procuring:
Sweet smelling, much delighting mans regard.
It seedes the eare, it amplifies the thought,
Except to those that know it, it is nought,
Briefly, sweet frend, I thinke of Alchymie,

As erst Thucidides the learned clarke,
Defynd a woman full of honestie:
(In plaine discourse, but not in riddles darke:)
That woman (said the sage) is best of all,
In whose dispraise, or praise, lesse speech is had,
That Alchymie say I is best of all,
Which few mens reasons can approue for bad:
Thus much of Alchymie, and thus an end,
Though thou commend not, frendly I commend.

THE PUBLISHED WORKS OF THOMAS LODGE IN CHRONOLOGICAL ORDER

C1580 Defence of Plays
1584 An Alarum against Usurers
1589 Scillaes Metamorphysis (reprinted in 1610 as A most pleasant Historie of Glaucus and Scilla)
1590 Rosalynde
1591 Robert, Second Duke of Normandy
1591 Catharos
1592 Euphues Shadow
1593 Phillis
1593 William Longbeard
1594 The Wounds of Civill War
1594 A Looking Glass for London (in collaboration with Robert Greene)
1595 A Fig for Momus
1596 The Divel coniured
1596 A Margarite of America
1596 Wits miserie
1596 Prosopopeia
1602 Paradoxes
1602 Works of Josephus
1603 A Treatise of the Plague
1614 The Workes of Seneca
1625 A Learned Summary of Du Bartas

www.ingramcontent.com/pod-product-compliance
Lightning Source LLC
Chambersburg PA
CBHW060102050426
42448CB00011B/2591